MAJOR WATERSHEDS OF IDAHO

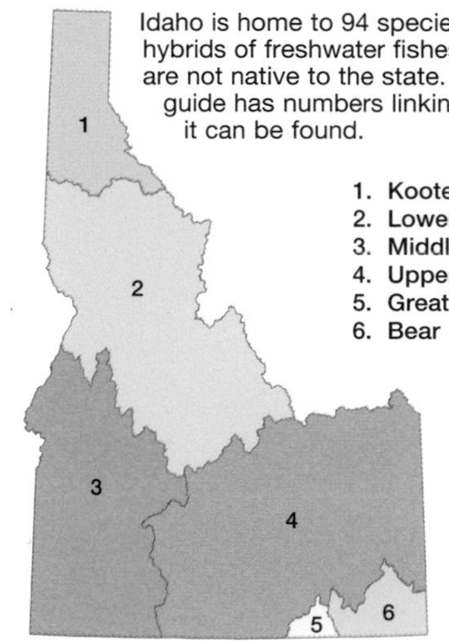

Idaho is home to 94 species and notable subspecies/hybrids of freshwater fishes. Approximately 50 species are not native to the state. Each fish species in the guide has numbers linking it to the watersheds where it can be found.

1. Kootenai-Pend Oreille-Spokane
2. Lower Snake
3. Middle Snake
4. Upper Snake
5. Great Salt Lake
6. Bear

HOW TO IDENTIFY FISHES

First, note the size, shape and color of the fish. Are there any distinguishing physical features like the double dorsal fins of the basses or the downturned lips of the suckers? Is the body thin or torpedo-shaped? Note the orientation and placement of fins on the body. Consult the text to confirm identification. A trip to your local fish market or aquarium is a good way to hone your skills at identifying fishes.

PARTS OF A FISH

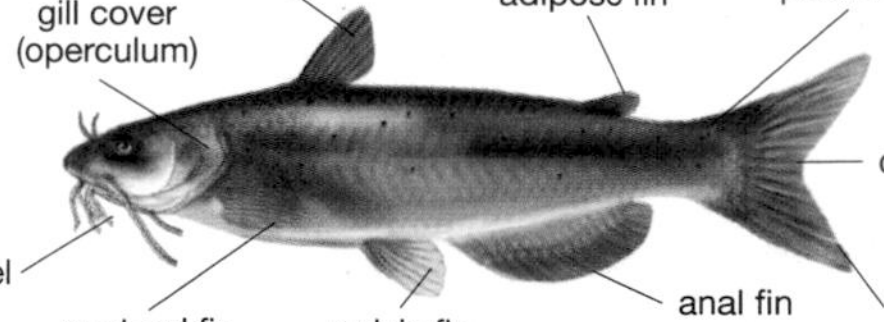

STATUS KEY

AS—Apparently Secure; CI—Critically Imperiled; H—Hybrid; I—Introduced; IM—Imperiled; I/N—invasive and native populations present; S—Secure; U—Uncertain; VU—Vulnerable

Made in the USA

Most illustrations show the adult male in breeding coloration. Colors and markings may be duller or absent during different seasons. The measurements denote the approximate maximum length of species documented in FishBase. Illustrations are not to scale.

Waterford Press publishes reference guides that introduce readers to nature observation, outdoor recreation and survival skills. **www.waterfordpress.com**

Dr. Matthew Morris is an evolutionary biologist. His current research uses genomics techniques to study the evolution of Threespine Stickleback.

Watershed map by Peter Peller, Geographic Information Systems Specialist.

ISBN 978-1-62005-564-9 $7.95 U.S.
UPC 8 84682 01509 1
10 9 8 7 6 5 4 3 2 1 2202701

IDAHO FRESHWATER FISHES

WATERFORD PRESS

A POCKET NATURALIST® GUIDE

IDAHO FRESHWATER FISHES

A Waterproof Folding Guide to Native and Introduced Species

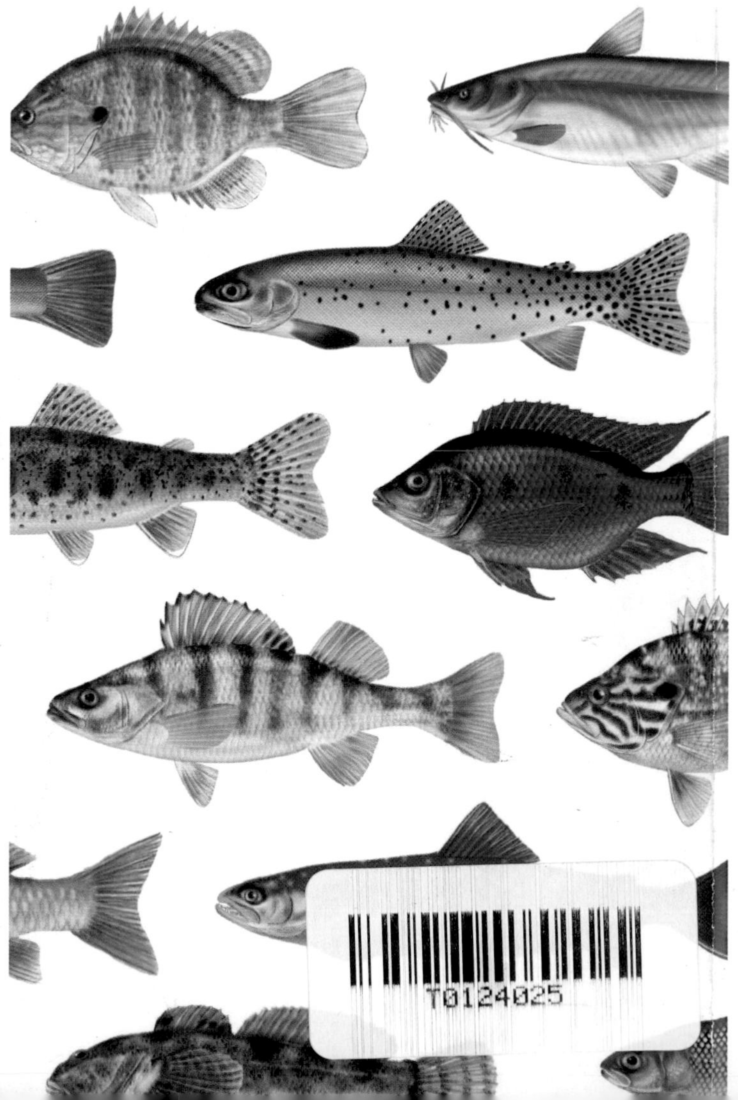

LAMPREYS, STURGEONS, SUCKERS

Lampreys (Petromyzontidae) – Long, eel-like body; circular sucking mouth. (1 sp.)

Pacific Lamprey
Entosphenus tridentatus
To 29.9 in. (76 cm)
Body is blue/brown with silver belly. Parasitic fish has 3 sharp upper teeth.

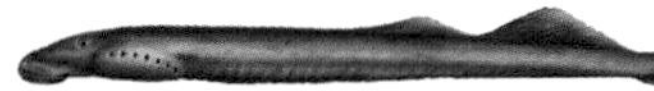

Basin #: 1, 2
Status: CI

Sturgeons (Acipenseridae) – Large armored scales; four barbels; caudal fin lobes of unequal length. (1 sp.)

White Sturgeon
Acipenser transmontanus
To 240.2 in. (610 cm)
Has gray back with 11-14 dorsal and 38-48 diamond-shaped lateral plates.

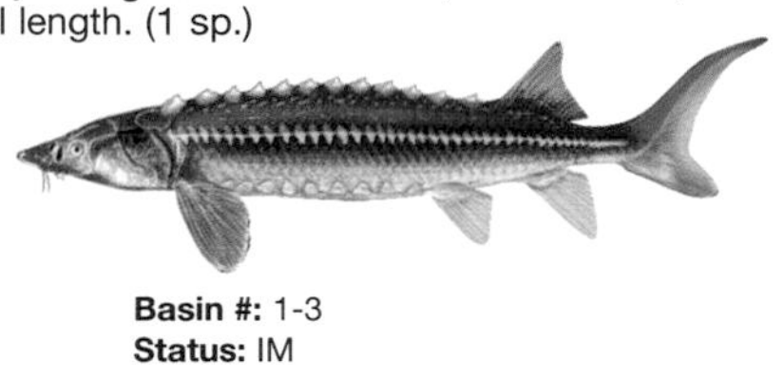

Basin #: 1-3
Status: IM

Suckers (Catostomidae) – Single dorsal fin overlaps pelvic fin; forked caudal fin; usually fleshy downturned lips. (6 spp.)

Longnose Sucker
Catostomus catostomus
To 25.2 in. (64 cm)
Long snout protrudes beyond lips.

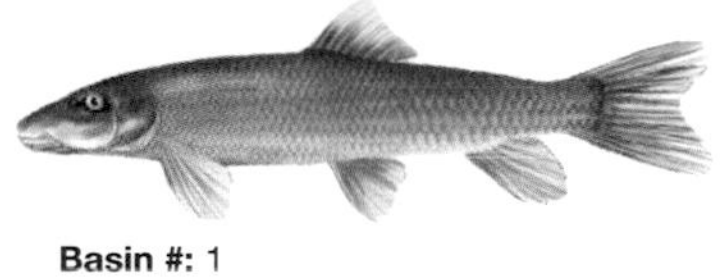

Basin #: 1
Status: VU

Utah Sucker
Catostomus ardens
To 25.6 in. (65 cm)
Membranes of dorsal fin are pigmented throughout.

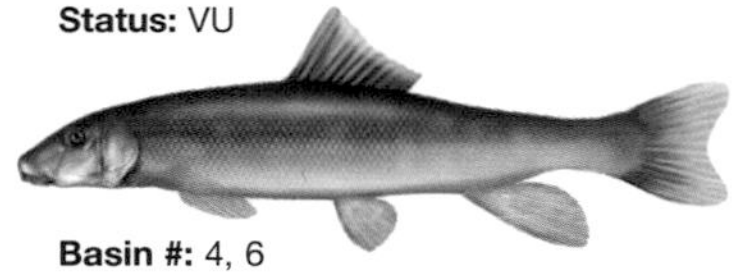

Basin #: 4, 6
Status: AS

Bridgelip Sucker
Catostomus columbianus
To 11.8 in. (30 cm)
Mouth has slight notch at corner, where lips meet.

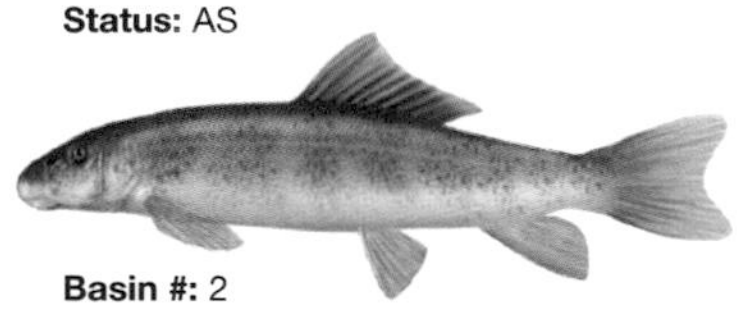

Basin #: 2
Status: AS

Largescale Sucker
Catostomus macrocheilus
To 24 in. (61 cm)
Snout does not protrude beyond lips. Dorsal fin membranes are speckled but not to edge.

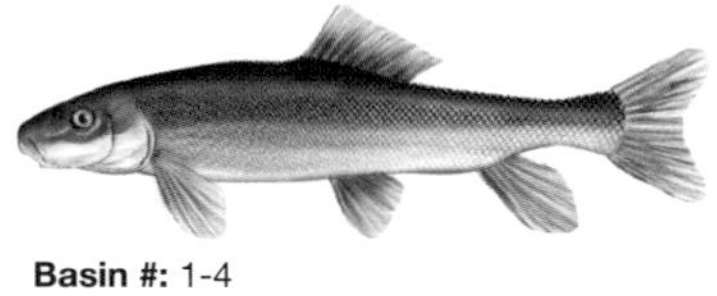

Basin #: 1-4
Status: AS

Cordilleran Sucker
Pantosteus bondi
To 5.1 in. (12.9 cm)
Has a distinct notch at the corner of the mouth where lips meet. Upper lip is smooth.

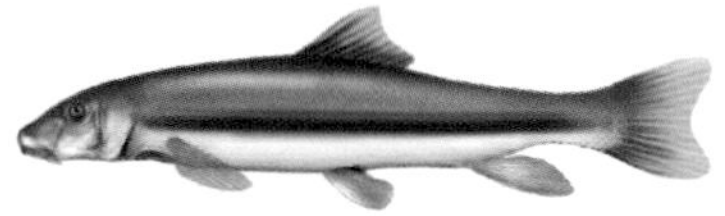

Basin #: 4-6
Status: AS

Green Sucker
Pantosteus virescens
To 16.1 in. (41 cm)
Head is blue. Genetically distinguished from Bluehead Sucker (*Pantosteus discobolus*), which is not found in Idaho.

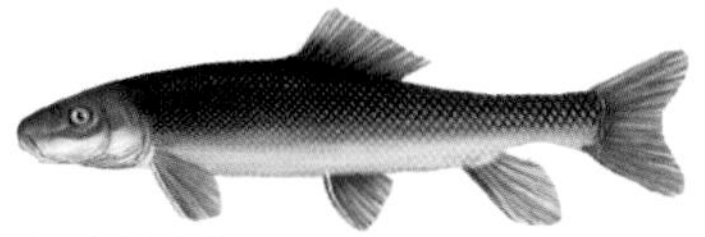

Basin #: 4-6
Status: VU

TENCHES, CARPS, TRUE MINNOWS, ETC.

Tenches (Tincidae) – Single dorsal fin overlaps pelvic fin; shallowly forked caudal fin. (1 sp.)

Tench
Tinca tinca
To 27.6 in. (70 cm)
Heavy fish looks laterally flattened. Eye is orange-red. Corner of mouth has a conspicuous barbel.

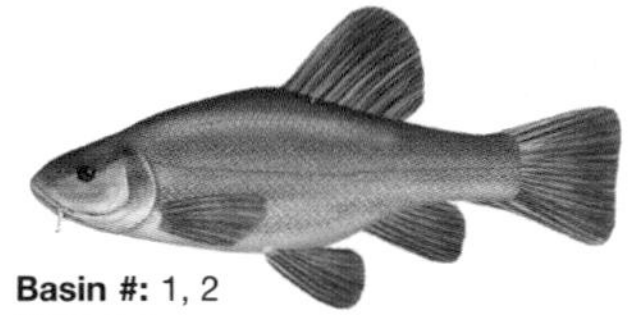

Basin #: 1, 2
Status: I

Carps (Cyprinidae) – Single dorsal fin typically does not overlap pelvic fin; forked caudal fin. (2 spp.)

Goldfish
Carassius auratus
To 18.9 in. (48 cm)
Has pointed snout and long convex dorsal fin. Released pets can breed in wild.

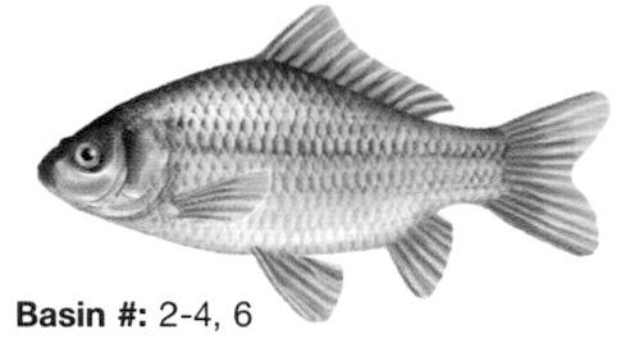

Basin #: 2-4, 6
Status: I

Common Carp
Cyprinus carpio
To 47.2 in. (120 cm)
Large-scaled fish has fleshy downturned lips and two pairs of barbels on upper jaw.

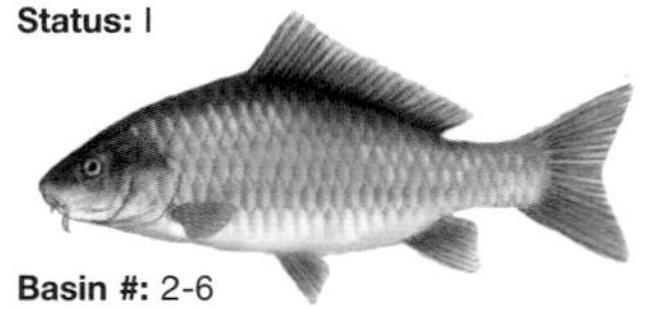

Basin #: 2-6
Status: I

East Asian Minnows (Xenocyprididae) – Single dorsal fin overlaps pelvic fin; forked caudal fin; forward-facing mouth. (1 sp.)

Grass Carp
Ctenopharyngodon idella
To 59.1 in. (150 cm)
Large brassy/gray body has large dark-edged scales and short dorsal fin. Typically sterile; introduced to control aquatic plants.

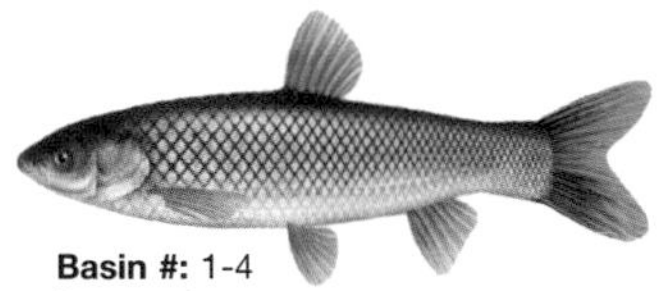

Basin #: 1-4
Status: I

True Minnows (Leuciscidae) – Single dorsal fin overlaps pelvic fin; forked caudal fin; (usually) forward-facing mouth. (14 spp.)

Chiselmouth
Gila alutacea
To 11.8 in. (30 cm)
Snout extends over mouth. Lower jaw is hard with chisel-like edge.

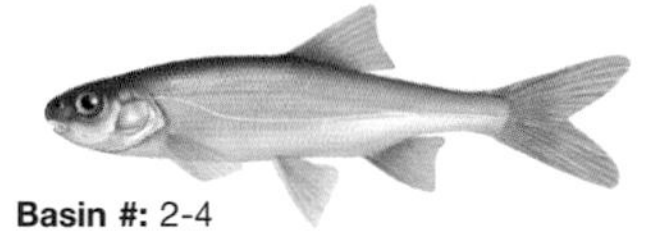

Basin #: 2-4
Status: AS

Utah Chub
Gila atraria
To 22 in. (56 cm)
Sides are yellow to brassy. Body is deep with blunt snout.

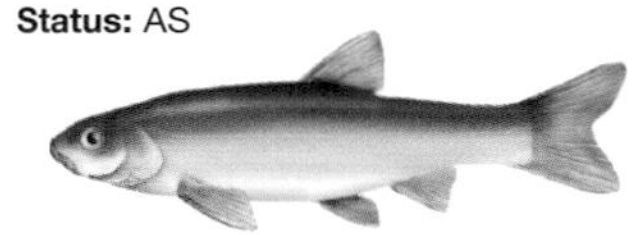

Basin #: 4-6
Status: AS

Northern Pikeminnow
Ptychocheilus oregonensis
To 24.8 in. (63 cm)
Largest North American minnow has a dark green back with white belly and a large mouth. Caudal fin is deeply forked.

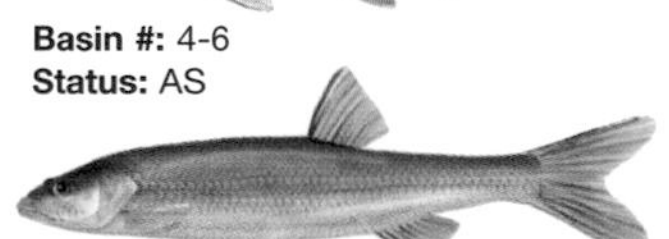

Basin #: 1-4
Status: AS

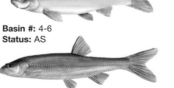

Northern Leatherside Chub
Lepidomeda copei
To 5.9 in. (15 cm)
Leathery body is covered in small scales. Back and sides are covered in black specks.

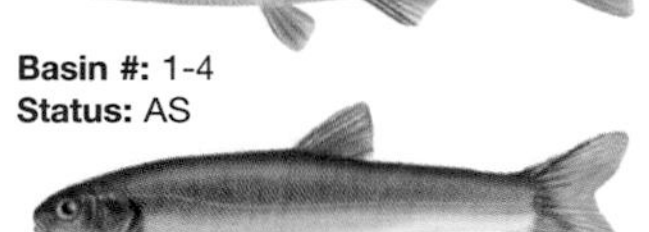

Basin #: 4
Status: IM

TRUE MINNOWS

True Minnows (Leuciscidae) – Cont'd.

Lake Chub
Couesius plumbeus
To 9.1 in. (23 cm)
Gray body has a black lateral stripe. Barbel is distinct in upper jaw. Orange 'pits' displayed in mature male only.

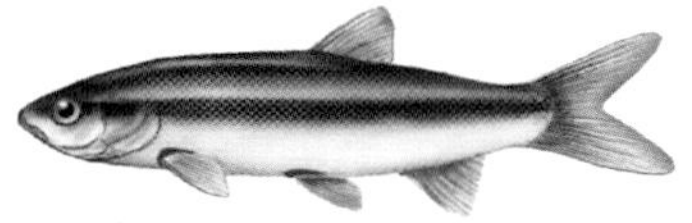

Basin #: 1
Status: VU

Fathead Minnow
Pimephales promelas
To 4 in. (10.1 cm)
Has a dorsal fin with a short 1st fin ray. Herringbone lines are present on sides. Breeding male has a black bumpy head.

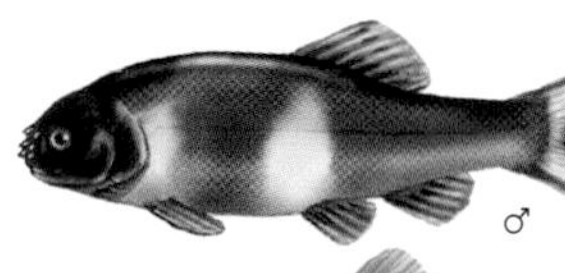

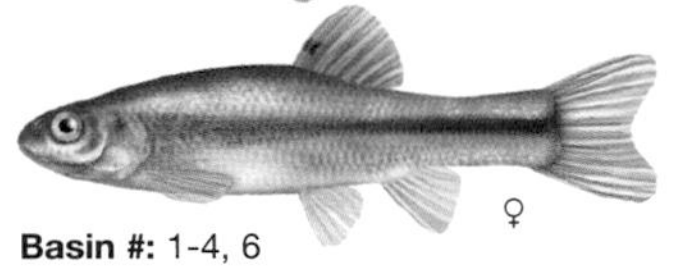

Basin #: 1-4, 6
Status: I

Peamouth
Mylocheilus caurinus
To 14.2 in. (36 cm)
Has two dark side stripes and a lower stripe ending at anal fin. Male has red on the sides and head.

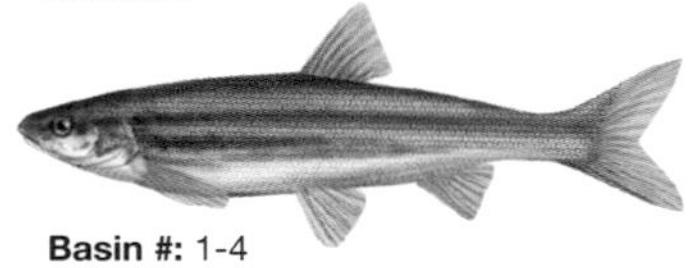

Basin #: 1-4
Status: VU

Longnose Dace
Rhinichthys cataractae
To 8.9 in. (22.5 cm)
Long snout extends past the mouth. Black stripe from snout to sides look like a moustache on smaller fish.

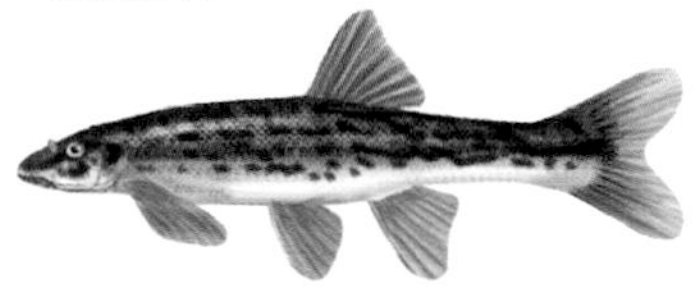

Basin #: 1-4, 6
Status: AS

Leopard Dace
Rhinichthys falcatus
To 4.7 in. (12 cm)
Dark irregular spots appear on sides and (sometimes) fins. Dorsal fin is sickle-shaped. Conspicuous barbel is present on corner of mouth.

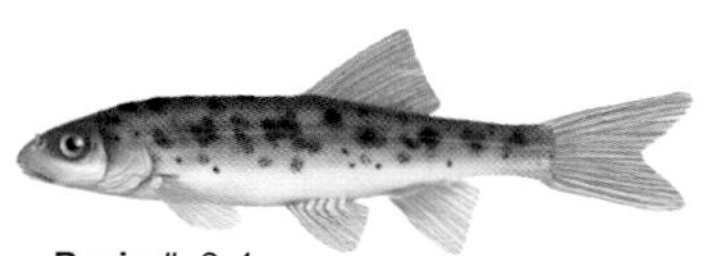

Basin #: 2-4
Status: VU

Speckled Dace
Rhinichthys osculus
To 4.3 in. (11 cm)
Highly variable species is gray with dark speckles. Mouth is terminal and sucker-like.

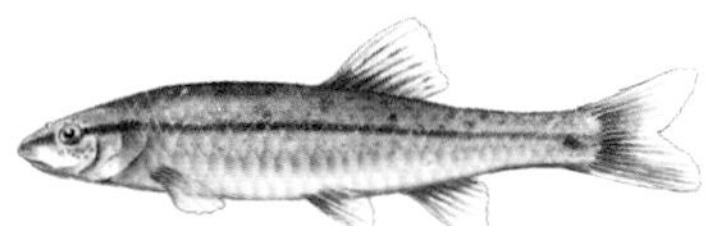

Basin #: 1-6
Status: S

Umatilla Dace
Rhinichthys umatilla
To 4.7 in. (12 cm)
Snout slightly overhangs mouth. Ancient hybrid of Leopard and Speckled Dace.

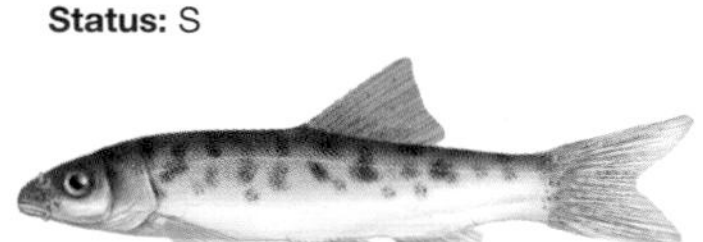

Basin #: 2, 3
Status: AS

Redside Shiner
Richardsonius balteatus
To 7.1 in. (18 cm)
Deep-bodied fish displays a black stripe, with yellow and red on the breeding male. Dorsal fin situated well after pelvic fin.

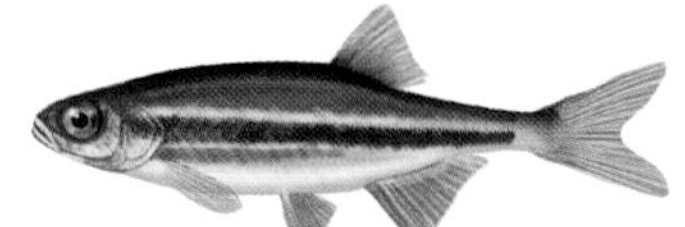

Basin #: 1-6
Status: S

NORTH AMERICAN CATFISHES, SHADS, PIKES

North American Catfishes (Ictaluridae) – Eight long barbels; single dorsal and adipose fin; smooth skin. (7 spp.)

Yellow Bullhead
Ameiurus natalis
To 23.6 in. (60 cm)
Dark or yellow body has white/yellow chin barbels and a long, straight anal fin. Caudal fin is slightly rounded.

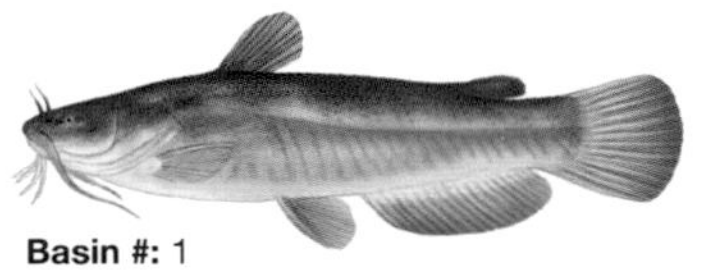

Basin #: 1
Status: I

Brown Bullhead
Ameiurus nebulosus
To 21.7 in. (55 cm)
Distinguished from introduced Black Bullhead (*Ameiurus melas*) by mottled body and dark (not pale) fin rays. Chin barbels are dark and caudal fin is slightly notched.

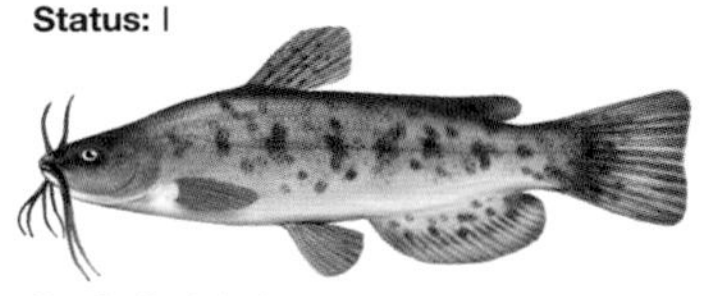

Basin #: 1-4, 6
Status: I

Blue Catfish
Ictalurus furcatus
To 65 in. (165 cm)
Bluish body displays no dark spots. Anal fin is straight and caudal fin is forked.

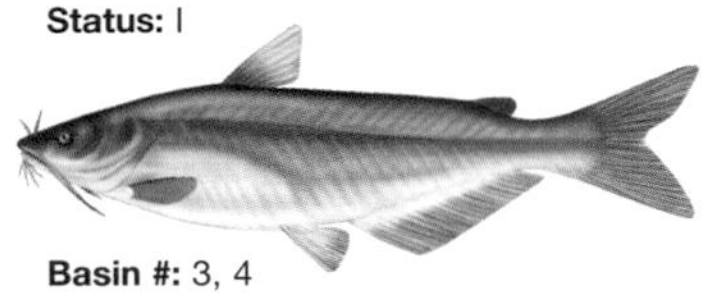

Basin #: 3, 4
Status: I

Channel Catfish
Ictalurus punctatus
To 52 in. (132 cm)
Silver body turns blue when large. Dark spots scattered on body are absent when large. Anal fin is rounded and caudal fin is deeply forked.

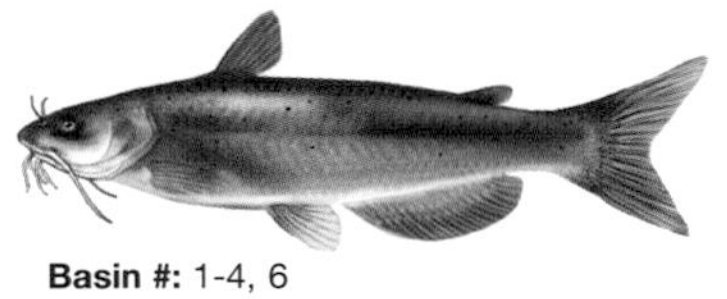

Basin #: 1-4, 6
Status: I

Tadpole Madtom
Noturus gyrinus
To 5.1 in. (13 cm)
Uniformly tan/gray body has a chubby tadpole shape. Vein-like projections appear on sides. The long adipose fin merges into a rounded caudal fin.

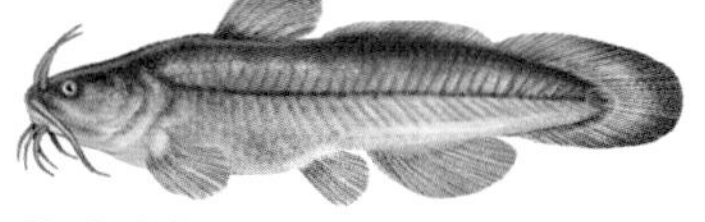

Basin #: 3
Status: I

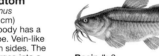

Flathead Catfish
Pylodictis olivaris
To 61 in. (155 cm)
Mottled body displays a flat head. Anal fin is short and rounded. Caudal fin is rounded or slightly notched, often with a white tip on upper lobe.

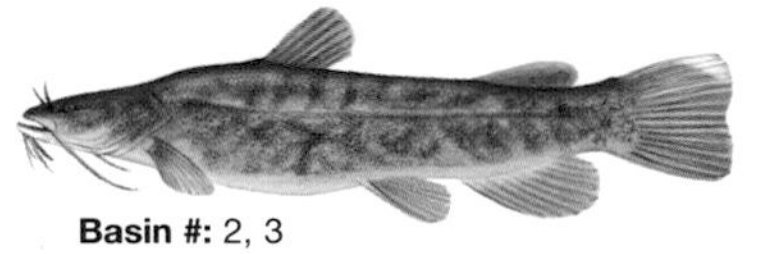

Basin #: 2, 3
Status: I

Herrings and Shads (Clupeidae) – Laterally compressed body; sawtooth belly; thick transparent skin covers eyes; single dorsal fin; forked caudal fin. (1 sp.)

American Shad
Alosa sapidissima
To 29.9 in. (76 cm)
Silver body has bluish-green back with large black spot behind gill cover, followed by 4-27 small dark spots.

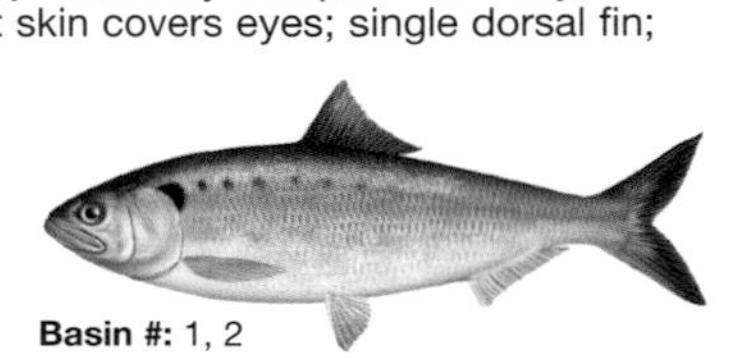

Basin #: 1, 2
Status: I

Pikes (Esocidae) – Long body and duck-like snout; single dorsal fin overlaps anal fin; forked caudal fin. (2 spp.)

Northern Pike
Esox lucius
To 59.1 in. (150 cm)
Light green body has white, horizontally oblong spots.

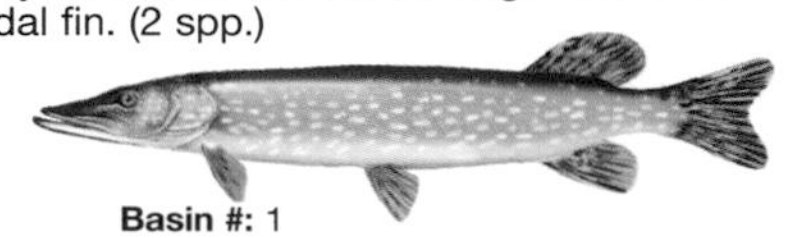

Basin #: 1
Status: I

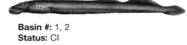

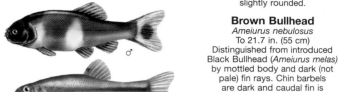

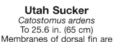

Whitefishes, Trouts & Salmons (Salmonidae) – Single dorsal and adipose fin; pectoral and pelvic fins do not overlap; spear-like axillary process at base of pelvic fin. (25 spp.)

Lake Whitefish
Coregonus clupeaformis
To 39.4 in. (100 cm)
Snout overhangs mouth. Body is silver with dorsal fin tip extending beyond base when folded back.

Basin #: 1
Status: I

Pygmy Whitefish
Prosopium coulteri
To 11 in. (28 cm)
Silver body has 7-14 dark, round parr (dark vertical) marks along all but the largest fish. Snout is blunt.

Basin #: 1
Status: AS

Mountain Whitefish
Prosopium williamsoni
To 27.6 in. (70 cm)
Body is silver, with 7-11 parr marks on juvenile. Dorsal fin tip does not extend beyond dorsal fin base when folded back.

Basin #: 1-4, 6
Status: S

Golden Trout
Oncorhynchus aguabonita
To 28 in. (71 cm)
Yellow-gold sides have a red stripe, cheeks and belly. Adult retains 10-12 purple parr marks. Black spots appear on back half of body.

Basin #: 1-4
Status: I

Rainbow Trout
Oncorhynchus mykiss
To 48 in. (122 cm)
Silver sides have a pink hue that may extend along the midline. Small black spots on the body and fins are arranged in lines on the caudal fin. Adipose fin has a black edge.

Basin #: 1-6
Status: I

Columbia River Redband Trout
Oncorhynchus mykiss gairdnerii
To 17.7 in. (45 cm)
Unlike the introduced Rainbow Trout of Idaho tends to keep parr marks into adulthood.

Basin #: 1-4
Status: AS

Westslope Cutthroat Trout
Oncorhynchus clarkii lewisi
To 20.5 in. (52 cm)
Colorful fish has a prominent red slash on either side of the lower jaw. Black spots are present on the body, especially toward the caudal fin. There are no black spots on the belly between pelvic and anal fins.

Basin #: 1, 2
Status: AS

Yellowstone Cutthroat Trout
Oncorhynchus clarkii bouvieri
To 21 in. (53.3 cm)
Has a prominent red slash on either side of the lower jaw. Medium-large, black spots are concentrated toward the caudal fin, with some on the belly. Coloration is drab.

Basin #: 4
Status: AS

Lahontan Cutthroat Trout
Oncorhynchus clarkii henshawi
To 39 in. (99 cm)
Largest North American trout has a pale red slash on either side of lower jaw. Black spots appear on sides of body and top of head.

Basin #: 3
Status: I

Whitefishes, Trouts & Salmons (Salmonidae) – Cont'd.

Kokanee
Oncorhynchus nerka
To 33.1 in. (84 cm)
This landlocked form of Sockeye Salmon has a blue back with silver sides. Few to no black spots are present.

Basin #: 3, 4
Status: U
nonbreeding

Chinook Salmon
Oncorhynchus tshawytscha
To 59.1 in. (150 cm)
Body has blue back with silver sides and black spots. Mouth is black with black gums. Species has declined in Idaho by 98%.

Basin #: 2
Status: U
nonbreeding

Coho Salmon
Oncorhynchus kisutch
To 42.5 in. (108 cm)
Body has blue back with silver sides and black spots. Black mouth has white gums. Extinct in Idaho since 1987; reintroduced through efforts of Nez Perce Tribe.

Basin #: 2
Status: I
nonbreeding

Arctic Char
Salvelinus alpinus
To 42.1 in. (107 cm)
Back and sides have pink spots. Dorsal and caudal fin have no spots. Caudal fin is forked.

Basin #: 2
Status: I

Bull Trout
Salvelinus confluentus
To 40.6 in. (103 cm)
Head is large and flat. Back and sides have small, pink to yellow spots. There are no spots on the dorsal or caudal fins. Caudal fin is slightly forked.

Basin #: 1-4
Status: AS

Brook Trout
Salvelinus fontinalis
To 33.9 in. (86 cm)
Red and white spots are surrounded by blue halos on the body. Worm-like markings appear on the back and dorsal fin. Caudal fin is notched or straight.

Basin #: 1-6
Status: I

Lake Trout
Salvelinus namaycush
To 59.1 in. (150 cm)
Deep-bodied fish is heavily spotted with white/yellow spots on a green-gray background. Caudal fin is deeply forked.

Basin #: 1-4, 6
Status: I

Brown Trout
Salmo trutta
To 55.1 in. (140 cm)
Robust fish has a light-brown body. Head and body have black and red spots, often extending below the lateral line. Caudal fin is square.

Basin #: 1-4, 6
Status: I

Arctic Grayling
Thymallus arcticus
To 29.9 in. (76 cm)
Silver body is marked by black spots toward the head. Distinctive for its sail-like dorsal fin. Caudal fin is forked.

Basin #: 1-4
Status: I

Burbots and Cuskfishes (Lotidae) – Long, eel-like body; single barbel on chin; rounded caudal fin. (1 sp.)

Burbot
Lota lota
To 59.8 in. (152 cm)
Smooth skin has dark mottling on a yellow background. 1st dorsal fin is short; 2nd dorsal fin is long.

Basin #: 1
Status: CI

Trout-Perches (Percopsidae) – Single dorsal and adipose fin; pectoral and pelvic fins overlap. (1 sp.)

Sand Roller
Percopsis transmontana
To 3.8 in. (9.6 cm)
Small, blue-green body has a large head. 8-13 dark spots appear along the lateral line. Back is arched.

Basin #: 2
Status: IM

Darters & Perches (Percidae) – Two dorsal fins usually unconnected; anal fin with no more than two spines. (4 spp.)

Yellow Perch
Perca flavescens
To 19.7 in. (50 cm)
Body is yellow-gold with 6-9 broad, vertical bands on each side.

Basin #: 1-6
Status: I

Sauger
Sander canadensis
To 29.9 in. (76 cm)
Body is large with a large mouth. Dorsal fin shows rows of dark spots.

Basin #: 6
Status: I

Walleye
Sander vitreus
To 42.1 in. (107 cm)
Body is large with a large mouth. Tip of the anal fin and lower lobe of the caudal fin are marked with a white spot.

Basin #: 1, 4, 6
Status: I

Loaches (Cobitidae) – Six barbels; rounded caudal fin; no adipose fin. (1 sp.)

Oriental Weatherfish
Misgurnus anguillicaudatus
To 11 in. (28 cm)
Eel-like body with fewer barbels than catfish. Dorsal fin is far back on body.

Basin #: 3
Status: I

Cichlids (Cichlidae) – Two dorsal fins connected; lateral line broken into two, with front portion placed higher on body (4 spp.)

Mozambique Tilapia
Oreochromis mossambicus
To 15.4 in. (39 cm)
Large mouth is obliquely angled. Yellow to gray sides have several black spots (or bars on the juvenile).

Basin #: 3, 4
Status: I

Livebearers (Poeciliidae) – Single dorsal fin; rounded caudal fin; no lateral line; upturned mouth; modified anal fin in males; females birth live young. (4 spp.)

Western Mosquitofish
Gambusia affinis
To 2.8 in. (7 cm)
Has dark patch below eye and rows of dark spots on caudal and dorsal fins.

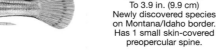

Basin #: 3, 4
Status: I

Sculpins (Cottidae) – Two dorsal fins; rounded caudal fin; pelvic fins near head and not fused together. (9 spp.)

Slimy Sculpin
Cottus cognatus
To 4.8 in. (12.1 cm)
Prickles displayed behind pectoral fin on head. Has 2-3 preopercular spines.

Basin #: 1
Status: VU

Torrent Sculpin
Cottus rhotheus
To 6.1 in. (15.5 cm)
Has narrow caudal peduncle and is heavily prickled on body and back. Has 3-4 preopercular spines.

Basin #: 1, 2
Status: VU

Mottled Sculpin
Cottus bairdii
To 5.9 in. (15 cm)
Note large head and dark spot on front and back of 1st dorsal fin. Prickles are behind the pectoral fin. Has 3 preopercular spines.

Basin #: 4, 6
Status: AS

Paiute Sculpin
Cottus beldingii
To 5.1 in. (13 cm)
Has no prickles and 1-2 preopercular spines.

Basin #: 2-6
Status: AS

Shoshone Sculpin
Cottus greenei
To 3.5 in. (9 cm)
Body is deep. Fish is unique to Thousand Springs formation.

Basin #: 4
Status: IM

Wood River Sculpin
Cottus leiopomus
To 4.3 in. (11 cm)
Has no prickles and 1 preopercular spine. Unique to Idaho.

Basin #: 3, 4
Status: IM

Shorthead Sculpin
Cottus confusus
To 5.9 in. (15 cm)
Prickles displayed behind pectoral fin. Has 2 preopercular spines.

Basin #: 1-4
Status: S

Cedar Sculpin
Cottus schitsuumsh
To 3.9 in. (9.9 cm)
Newly discovered species on Montana/Idaho border. Has 1 small skin-covered preopercular spine.

Basin #: 1
Status: U

Basses & Sunfishes (Centrarchidae) – Two dorsal fins merged into one; anal fin with at least three spines. (8 spp.)

White Crappie
Pomoxis annularis
To 20.9 in. (53 cm)
Body is pale with broken vertical dark bars. Dorsal fin has 5-6 spines. First dorsal spine is much shorter than the last.

Basin #: 1-6
Status: I

Black Crappie
Pomoxis nigromaculatus
To 19.3 in. (49 cm)
Side has black blotches present. Dorsal fin has 7-8 spines. First dorsal spine is much shorter than the last.

Basin #: 1-4, 6
Status: I

Green Sunfish
Lepomis cyanellus
To 12.2 in. (31 cm)
Blue spots on narrow dark body form lines. Black opercular flap is edged with red/yellow. Mouth is large and blue wiggles are on operculum.

Basin #: 1, 3, 4, 6
Status: I

Pumpkinseed
Lepomis gibbosus
To 15.7 in. (40 cm)
Round orange and blue body has orange and blue stripes alternating on operculum. Black opercular flap is relatively short and straight, with a red tip.

Basin #: 1-4
Status: I

Warmouth
Lepomis gulosus
To 12.2 in. (31 cm)
Stripes radiate back from red eye. Black opercular flap is short with yellow edge and red spot. Side has 6-11 bars.

Basin #: 3
Status: I

Bluegill
Lepomis macrochirus
To 16.1 in. (41 cm)
Round dark body has blue operculum and black opercular flap. Vertical faded stripes are present along body.

Basin #: 1-4, 6
Status: I

Smallmouth Bass
Micropterus dolomieu
To 27.2 in. (69 cm)
Olive-green body has 8-16 bars on each side. Dorsal fins are clearly connected. Upper jaw does not extend past the eye.

Basin #: 1-4, 6
Status: I

Largemouth Bass
Micropterus salmoides
To 38.2 in. (97 cm)
Olive-green body has black (often marked) stripe along sides. Dorsal fins are only slightly connected. Upper jaw extends past the eye.

Basin #: 1-6
Status: I

Bear Lake, shared between the Southeast corner of Idaho and northern Nevada, contains five species or subspecies of fishes found nowhere else in the world, including four members of Salmonidae (Whitefishes, Trouts & Salmons) and one of Cottidae (Sculpins).

Bear Lake Whitefish
Prosopium abyssicola
To 11 in. (28 cm)
Silver-white body is free of spots and has a blunt snout.

Basin #: 6
Status: CI

Bonneville Cisco
Prosopium gemmifer
To 8.7 in. (22 cm)
Back is greenish. Sides are silvery to brassy. Snout is pointed and elongated.

Basin #: 6
Status: VU

Bonneville Whitefish
Prosopium spilonotus
To 22 in. (56 cm)
Body is silver-white and spots are present on the juvenile. Snout is very blunt.

Basin #: 6
Status: VU

Bonneville Cutthroat Trout
Oncorhynchus clarkii utah
To 10 in. (25.5 cm)
Similar to Westslope Cutthroat Trout, but pale parr marks are present on yellow body. Successfully transplanted elsewhere.

Basin #: 5, 6
Status: AS

Bear Lake Sculpin
Cottus extensus
To 5.1 in. (13 cm)
Two dorsal fins are separated. Heavily prickled, except on underside. Has 3 preopercular spines.

Basin #: 6
Status: VU

Idaho is home to several other introduced species, including Tui Chub, Spottail Shiner, Atlantic Salmon, Redbelly Tilapia, Blue Tilapia, Convict Cichlid, Shortfin Molly, Guppy, and Green Swordtail and one member of the family Osmeridae, the Rainbow Smelt. Hybrids are also intentionally released, including Saugeye (Walleye x Sauger), Splake (Brook Trout x Lake Trout), Tiger Trout (Brown Trout x Brook Trout), and Tiger Muskellunge (Muskellunge x Northern Pike).